French Holidays & Traditions

G000153825

FRENCH HOLIDAYS & TRADITIONS

Margo Lestz

This book is part of the Curious Histories series.

ISBN: 978-0-9931371-1-2

Published by
Boo-Tickety Publishing
London

Contents

Introduction

This book is made up of twelve chapters – one for each month of the year, and each chapter contains one or two stories. These stories might relate to a holiday observed during that month, or they could relate to a tradition which may not be associated with any particular date. At the end of each chapter there is a list of holidays and observances for that month.

You might be surprised to learn that there are only eleven public holidays per year in France. If you've spent much time there, you might be wondering why it seems like there are so many more. One reason is that there are many observances which are not public holidays but are still occasions to celebrate something, and they usually involve a special tradition.

However, the main reason that it seems there are so many holidays is that the French have mastered the art of "bridge building". Faire le pont, which literally means "to make the bridge", is the term the French use for their clever way of stretching a one-day holiday into a four-day weekend. If a public holiday happens to fall on a Tuesday or Thursday, the French "make the bridge" and take the adjoining Monday or Friday off as well, resulting in four consecutive days off work. If a holiday falls on a Monday or Friday, they can only stretch it into a three-day weekend. And it's bad news for everyone when a holiday lands on a Wednesday or, even worse, on a weekend!

In perusing the list of French public holidays, you might wonder why some religious holidays are listed. After all, France prides itself on keeping the church and state completely separate. Well, the ever-practical French would never dream of wasting a perfectly good holiday. And, besides, most of the traditions around these holidays existed before Christianity and have woven their way deep into French culture. The four religious holidays that have become public holidays are the Assumption, Christmas, Ascension and All Saints' Day.

Note from the author:
I hope this book will bring you enjoyment and a deeper understanding of some facets of the complex French culture. As a disclaimer, I have to say that in France, as in many countries, traditions vary from region to region and even from family to family. I've done my best to research and observe what I see around me in the south of France, but in a land of two hundred and forty-six different kinds of cheese, I'm sure there are many variations of all these traditions.

Happy Reading! – Bonne lecture!

JANUARY

Janvier

There's a Bean in My Cake!

Epiphany - The Celebration of Kings

If you're in France in January and eating a piece of pie or cake, chew carefully. One French tradition could cost you a tooth if you're not paying attention.

In January, the French eat a special dessert called a *galette des rois* which contains a little baked-in trinket. This dessert comes in two versions: one form is similar to a pie, with a flaky crust and an almond filling, and the other is more like a brioche. But both are called *galette des rois* (or king cake), and both can be hazardous to the teeth of an uninformed diner.

To discover how this custom of hiding items in cakes began, we have to go back to Roman times and to their winter solstice celebration. They would bake a large loaf of bread with a bean inside it, and the person who found the bean was crowned king for the day.

The Christian church changed the solstice celebration to the Epiphany and fixed the date as the 6th of January. With the "king for a day" theme already established, it became the time to remember the Biblical kings who had presented gifts to the baby Jesus. Over the years, the "bean-in-the-bread" turned into a "bean-in-the-cake" and the cake became known as the *galette des rois*, or king cake.

In sixteenth-century Paris, this cake found itself at the centre of a conflict between the *boulangeries* (or bakeries) and the *pâtisseries* (or cake shops). They each wanted the sole right to make and sell this special cake with the hidden bean. The cake shops won and the bakeries were forbidden to make the cakes. But the bakeries weren't about to give up so easily. If they were forbidden to make king cakes, then they would simply make king *pies*. And that is why today there are two distinct versions of the king cake.

Traditionally, the pie version has been preferred in the north of France and the brioche version in the south. But today you're likely to pass a bakery window and see both versions displayed side by side (at least in the south of France).

The "Bakery vs Cake Shop War" wasn't the only problem caused by this innocent-looking cake with its hidden bean. After the French Revolution, in which Louis XVI, the king of France, lost his head, the new leaders of the country wanted to make the king cake illegal. They had just got rid of one king and didn't want another one – not even a pretend one. They were seriously considering outlawing the token king custom and arresting anyone who dared to make or sell the king cakes. But after considering the possible public reaction, they came to their senses. They realised that you just don't mess with a Frenchman's food or holidays, so the cake with the bean was safe.

The bean is called a *fève* in French. Technically, a *fève* is a broad bean, which was the original king selector. But, at the end of the nineteenth century, the beans were replaced by porcelain figurines. (I can't help but think that dentists must have come up with that idea.) Even though the trinkets in the cake are no longer beans, they are still called *fèves* and they come in a variety of forms. They might be tiny *santons* (nativity figures), cartoon characters, or any number of other things. Some people collect these *fèves*, and there is even a *fève* museum in the city of Blain.

Eating cake with a baked-in *fève* is an ancient tradition which is still popular today. At January gatherings, when it's time to serve the cake, the youngest child gets under the table. The hostess cuts the cake into as many pieces as there are diners, then she ask the child, "Who is this piece for?" The child calls out a name and the cake is distributed according to his instructions. This way there can be no cheating, as he can't see the *fève* and play favourites. Everyone chews their piece of cake slowly, to avoid cracking a tooth, until the *fève* is found.

The lucky person who finds the trinket in his cake becomes the king (or queen) for the day. He gets to wear a paper crown which is supplied with the cake. The king's royal responsibility, after choosing his queen, might be to bring another king cake to the next gathering – and that could be the following week, because the French eat these cakes for weeks (in the south). This way, everyone gets a chance to find the *fève*, wear the crown, and be king or queen of the party.

The only person in all of France who does not have the opportunity to find the *fève* and become king for the day is the President of the Republic of France. Each year the bakers' association presents the President with a giant *galette des rois* – but with one important difference: there is no *fève* inside, and no crown accompanies it. The French dethroned their king a long time ago, and they're not taking any chances!

~ *French Joke* ~
A man goes to the dentist and says, "I broke a tooth on the fève in the king cake."
The dentist says, "Well, since you're the king, you're going to need a crown."

January Dates
and Events

1st January – New Year's Day (*Le jour de l'An*)
Le jour de l'An, which literally translates as "the day of the year", is a public holiday. The proper New Year's greeting is *bonne année* and it shouldn't be said before the 1st of January. Once New Year's Day rolls around, however, you can carry on wishing people *bonne année* all month long – but you should say it to each person only once, the first time you see them in the new year.

6th January – Epiphany (*La Fête des Rois*)
La Fête des Rois, or "the celebration of kings", is not a public holiday, but a religious and traditional one. Today, it's celebrated by eating lots of cake and wearing paper crowns (if you find the "bean").

Winter Sales (*Les Soldes*)
January is a month of sales in France and you will see signs for the *soldes* in all the shop windows. The

winter sales start in January and run for five weeks. Then the summer sales start at the end of June and run for five weeks. These two sales events (summer and winter) are the main sales of the year. The exact dates are regulated by the government and can change from year to year.

Since 2009, the shops have had the right to an additional two weeks of floating sales, or *soldes flottants*. They can use these two weeks together or separately. However, these floating sales are not allowed in the month before the regular five weeks of sales.

FEBRUARY

Février

Carnival Kings, Silly Strings and Blooming Things

It's Carnival Time in Nice

The carnival celebration, like many other French holidays, came from Catholic religious observances. Many cities all over France have carnival festivities, and here is the story of one of the larger and older ones, in Nice, France.

The Nice carnival always includes a royal visit. Every year at carnival time, a different king comes to town to celebrate the carnival with the people of Nice and to participate in the parades on his own special float. But it wasn't always this way...

Kings and Parades

In the beginning, there wasn't a parade in sight and the carnival resembled a big disorganised street party. But in 1830, when the King and Queen of Sardinia (Charles-Félix and Marie-Christine) were in Nice, the city wanted to do something special, so the first carnival parade was organised in their honour. The royal couple sat on their palace balcony and waved the *royal wave* as prominent Niçois ladies and gentlemen, dressed in elegant costumes, filed past in decorated carriages.

That parade was such a success that the next year, when the king wasn't present, the Niçois took some straw and old clothes and made themselves a king. They placed him on the palace balcony, where he approvingly watched the passing revelry. Then in 1882 they decided that this mock king should participate in the procession.

Do you think anyone will notice that he's not the real king?

Happy Carnival

I don't think so... Keeping that crown from the king cake was a good idea!

This was the beginnings of the modern Nice carnival parade, which is always presided over by a gigantic kingly character. His arrival on the royal float signals the beginning of the festivities. Each year brings a different king who sets the theme for the entire event. For example, if

His Majesty, King of Gastronomy, presides, then all of the floats will have something to do with food. Unfortunately for His Royal Highness, his reign is very short-lived. France isn't known for being merciful to its kings and on the last night of the carnival, he's put out to sea on a little boat and burned while the carnival-goers celebrate with fireworks.

Even though His Majesty doesn't have much time in Nice, he has a full schedule. For more than two weeks, there are parades every day and evening. He oversees the line of decorated floats, interspersed with marching bands and costumed characters, as it makes its way along the carnival route. The King's helpers (the people on the floats) throw confetti and candies into the crowd, and in return they are targeted by children with cans of silly string.

Silly String and other Projectiles

One thing you can't escape at the carnival is silly string (that aerosol spray that sends out foamy streamers that stick to everything but are easy to remove). It can be annoying, but it's actually the modern version of, and an improvement upon, a long-standing tradition. In the earliest carnivals, people threw things at each other: things like sugar-coated seeds, confetti made of plaster, egg shells filled

I sure wish someone would hurry up and invent silly string!

with soot or flour, rotten eggs, fruit and vegetables. Those who had a window overlooking the parade route stocked up with "ammunition" and bombarded those in the streets below.

The masks and costumes worn during the carnival were not only to hide your identity, but also to protect your face and clothing from all of the objects flying through the air. Some masks were even made of iron for extra protection. In our day, throwing eggs, vegetables and plaster has, thankfully, fallen out of fashion, leaving us with harmless paper confetti and silly string. Now, many people even feel brave enough to attend the carnival "maskless".

Flower Battles

While those early rowdy, egg-throwing free-for-alls were taking place in the Old Town of Nice, another more genteel battle was born on the seaside promenade. In 1876 the first *bataille de fleurs* (or flower battle) took place. It was an elegant parade of carriages covered in flowers and was reserved for the elite, who didn't like getting hit with eggs and vegetables. This is where Queen Victoria is said to have thrown flowers at young soldiers. It was more of a show with polite flower exchanges – not really much of a battle.

The modern "flower battle" in Nice is still a separate event from the carnival parade. A procession of bloom-covered floats rolls along the seaside promenade, showcasing the variety of flowers grown in the region. Each float is manned by beautifully costumed ladies showering the admiring crowd with colourful blossoms. Today, the spectators don't normally throw things back at them, but they are sometimes attacked by a child with a can of silly string.

Even though the Nice carnival has changed over the years, it has retained three essential historical ingredients: a king to preside over the parade, good-natured battles, and lots of blooming flowers.

A few interesting facts about the Nice carnival

- The Nice Carnival is one of the oldest in Europe. The first written mention of it is from 1294 when a count of Provence wrote that he had spent the "joyous days of carnival" in Nice.
- It inspired the carnival in Rio de Janeiro which was developed after Emperor Pedro II was in Nice for the carnival of 1888.
- In 1890 after a prominent member of the Valley Hunt Club of Pasadena saw the Flower Battle in Nice, he proposed one for his area and the *Tournament of Roses* was born.

February Dates and Events

2nd February – Candlemas (*La Chandeleur*)
La Chandeleur is a religious and traditional holiday which takes place forty days after Christmas and is meant to commemorate the date when Jesus was first presented in the temple. Today the French celebrate this day by eating lots of *crêpes*.

If you want to have good luck in the coming year, you need to make some *crêpes* on the 2nd of February. While holding a coin in your left hand, hold the pan in your right and try to flip the *crêpe*. If you're successful and the *crêpe* makes a nice landing in the pan, you'll have good fortune. If not.... well, just try again.

Another *crêpe* tradition says that, to ensure a good harvest, you should not eat the first *crêpe* you make, but put it in a cupboard and leave it there all year. Unless you are a farmer, you probably don't want to try this one. The *crêpes* that don't end up in the cupboard are usually enjoyed with cider or apple juice.

14th February – Valentine's Day (*La Saint-Valentin*)

Valentine's Day is celebrated in France, as in many places, by giving chocolate and flowers to your loved one and being very romantic.

The following dates are dependent upon the date of Easter, which changes every year, but they often fall in February:

Carnival (*Le Carnaval*)

The starting date of carnival festivities can vary but Carnival should end on Fat Tuesday, or *Mardi Gras*, which is forty-seven days before Easter. Carnival celebrations are held in many cities throughout France.

Note: In France the carnival celebration is not referred to as *Mardi Gras*, as it is in some other places (such as New Orleans). *Mardi Gras* is literally translated as "Fat Tuesday" and is the day before Ash Wednesday, which is the start of Lent.

Fat Tuesday and Ash Wednesday (*Mardi Gras et Le Mercredi des Cendres*)

Mardi Gras, or Fat Tuesday, is forty-seven days before Easter so it falls on a different date each year (but always on a Tuesday) between the 3rd of February and the 9th of March. Traditionally, there was a seven-day period of partying (Carnival) and eating up all the food that was not allowed during Lent, including meats and fatty foods. The last day of this feasting was *Mardi Gras*, or

Fat Tuesday. The next day is Ash Wednesday or *Mercredi des Cendres* which is the first day of Lent.

Today, *Mardi Gras* is celebrated by eating *crêpes* (yes, more *crêpes*) and *beignets*. *Beignets* are a fried pastry that can have various flavours, shapes and even names depending on the area of France. There are at least nineteen different names for this tasty treat. Traditionally, *crêpes* and *beignets* were made to use up all the remaining oil, butter and eggs before Lent. Today, they are usually made just because they taste good.

MARCH

Mars

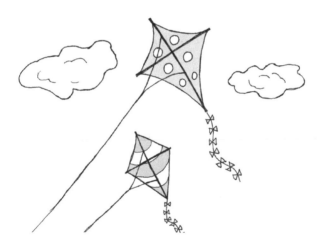

Easter Bunny
versus
Easter Bell

Easter Egg Deliveries

If you thought the folkloric characters from your childhood were universal, you would be wrong. Take, for example, the bunny that hops around delivering eggs at Easter time. He visits many children in many countries, but he doesn't hop over to France. But fear not, the French have come up with another way to distribute Easter eggs to their children.

First, let's talk about Easter in the lands of the Easter Bunny. In those regions, children decorate hard-boiled eggs which are left out in plain sight the night before Easter so the bunny won't have any trouble finding them. Then everyone goes to bed.

The Easter Bunny

A rabbit that hops into your home, hides eggs, and leaves chocolate.

While they sleep, the Easter Bunny comes, sneaks into the house and hides all the eggs. He might stash them outside on the lawn, in trees, in the house – anywhere. Then before hopping away, he leaves a basket full of sweets, including chocolate eggs, chocolate bunnies, chocolate chickens, chocolate... Well, you get the idea.

When the children wake up the next morning, they find their basket of goodies, nibble a little pre-breakfast chocolate, and then go on a hunt for the eggs the rabbit has hidden. Over the next week they crack open the decorated shells and eat the hard-boiled eggs – but only after all of the chocolate is gone, of course.

If you think it's strange that a rabbit would hop around to every house once a year to hide the eggs the children have decorated and leave them a basket of chocolate, wait until you hear what happens in France.

France is outside the Easter Bunny's delivery zone – except in the north-east, close to the German border. There, children make little nests which they place in the garden. During the night, the German Easter Bunny hops across the border and fills them with Easter eggs. Otherwise, a French Easter goes something like this:

On the Thursday night before Easter, all the church bells go silent – and they won't be heard from again until Easter Sunday. Why? Well, this is the interesting part. They sprout wings, pack up their suitcases and fly off to Rome. It's said that they go to Rome to visit the Pope, but I imagine they probably have enough time to do a little sight-seeing or fly around to Italian bell towers visiting relatives as well. But what they do in their private time isn't our concern here.

After their Vatican visit, they apparently go to the market, where they load up their bags with chocolate. Chocolate eggs, chocolate rabbits, chocolate chicks and chocolate bells (in their honour, of course). The chocolate April Fool's fish are usually in the shops at that time so they throw those in too – they do double duty as Easter fish.

As the bells make their way back to France and to their respective steeples on Easter eve, they drop these chocolatey treats at the houses of children along their flight path. Even though they have a long night of deliveries, they have to be up bright and early the next morning to ring in Easter Sunday. When the children hear the bells ringing, they run outside to hunt for the goodies that the *Cloches de Pâques*, or Easter Bells, have left them.

This Easter Bell egg-delivery system is an interesting idea, but how does it compare with the Easter Bunny? Bunnies are cute: they hop and wiggle their noses, while bells are cold and not very cuddly. You have to admit, though, that growing wings and flying to Rome is a pretty impressive trick.

Even though the two methods of dispensing Easter treats are very different, does it really matter? Both techniques supply one of the essential ingredients of Easter – lots of chocolate!

The Easter Bell

A bell that sprouts wings, flies over your home, and drops chocolate.

It Pays to be Polite in France

A Tradition of Politeness

Politeness is a deep-rooted and sometimes misinterpreted tradition in French culture. Misunderstandings often arise because countries have different ideas about what constitutes good manners. In France it's the *words of politeness* that are very important, maybe even more important than the attitude of the person saying them.

As an example, in one café in France, minding your manners can significantly reduce the price of your coffee. The menu reads:

A cup of coffee – € 7.00
A cup of coffee, *please* – € 4.25
Hello, a cup of coffee, *please* – € 1.40

Of course, this is meant as a humorous way to remind customers to be polite, but it's a great illustration of the French attitude toward good manners.

In France the courtesy words and phrases are very important and NOT optional. Fortunately, they're easy to master, but if you can't manage them in French, at least say them in English. More than likely, the French will understand you and think that you're a polite person who doesn't speak French – which is, of course, much better than being thought of as a rude person who doesn't speak French. So if you want to be polite in France (and I'm sure you do), here are some easy words and phrases (along with my attempt at phonetic pronunciation) to help you on your way:

Hello and Goodbye

- *Bonjour* (bon zhure) – hello: As you can see from the coffee example above, greeting someone before placing an order or asking a question is much more important in France than in some other countries. (Plus being polite can save you €5.60 on a coffee!) In France, you should never approach a sales person and immediately ask a question. Always start with a polite greeting: "*Bonjour*" or, even better, "*Bonjour, Madame*" or "*Bonjour, Monsieur*". Then you can ask your question. I have to admit to having committed this error myself once (or twice). I was in a hurry and just went up to a clerk and blurted out my request. She looked at me and slowly said "*Bonjour, Madame*" in a tone that said, "Did we

leave our manners at home this morning?"
(Ouch!) Then, of course, I had to say "*Bonjour,
Madame*" and start again with my question. So it
just saves time (and embarrassment) to remember
to greet people first. You should also say "*bonjour*"
when you enter a shop. You don't need to direct
it to anyone in particular, just a general *bonjour*
will do. When I go into a shop, I say "*bonjour*",
even if I don't see anyone there, because I'm sure
there is someone somewhere watching to see how
polite I am.

- *Bonsoir* (bon swa) – **good evening:** At a certain
  point during the afternoon, *bonjour* will become
  bonsoir. There is no precise hour when this
  occurs, and it's not a big deal if you say *bonjour*
  instead of *bonsoir*. But if someone greets you with
  bonsoir you can reply with *bonsoir*.

- *Au revoir* (oh rev wa) – **goodbye:** Just as it's polite to say *bonjour* when arriving, you should say *au revoir* when leaving. When exiting a shop, say "*Merci, au revoir*".

Please and Thank You

These are magic words in many cultures.
- *S'il vous plaît* (seel voo play) – **please:** This is very important; just add it to the end of every request.
- *Merci* (mer see) – **thank you:** It's good manners everywhere to thank people when they do something for you.
- *Je vous en prie* (zhuh voo zon pree) – **you're welcome:** This is the standard response when someone thanks you. That might be a bit of a mouthful if you don't speak French, but depending on the situation you might also use:
  - *Merci à vous* (mer see ah voo) – **thank YOU** (returning the thanks to the other person).
  - *Avec plaisir* (aveck play zir) – **it was my pleasure.**
  - But often, just a smile and a nod will be sufficient.

By using just these few words and phrases, you will have the French marvelling at what a well-mannered person you are. But if you really want to make a good impression, here are a few other things to be aware of:

Cultural Differences

- **Do you speak English?** Don't assume that everyone speaks English. What would you think if you were in your home town and a French tourist approached and just started asking you questions in French? You might think they were a bit rude, no? So start with a *bonjour* – even if it's badly pronounced. Then ask, "Do you speak English?" If they don't understand, then you have your answer. But they will probably say "a little bit" and then try to help you in English.
- **Wait to be seated** in restaurants.
- **Ask for the bill.** Normally the waiter will not bring the bill until you ask for it because it's not polite to hurry customers. So when you are ready, ask for *"l'addition, s'il vous plaît"* (la dee shon, seel voo play).
- **Tone it down.** In general, the French are a quiet bunch. Talk and laugh at a moderate volume.
- **Don't take up more space than you need.** If you are a party of two, don't take a table for four – even if there are lots of empty tables. Don't take up the entire pavement.
- **Put money on the counter** instead of handing it to the person you are paying. Of course, there are exceptions. If the person holds out their hand, by all means give them the money, but generally it's more polite to place it on the counter.
- **Keep your cool.** Hopefully you won't have any major problems, but sometimes things can go

wrong. Normally (if you have been polite) you will find the French to be very helpful. But be warned: you will get nowhere by demanding your rights, yelling or asking to see a manager. (The "customer is always right" philosophy has not caught on in France, and managers stick up for their employees.) If you want to be helped, you must, above all, remain calm and polite.

So there you have it, the secrets of French politeness – and how not to overpay for a cup of coffee.

March Dates
and Events

There are no fixed holidays in March, but Easter often falls in this month.

 Easter (*Pâques*)
Easter is a religious holiday that falls on a Sunday between the 22nd of March and the 25th of April. The date varies from year to year because it's based on the lunar calendar. In France, apart from the religious observations, it's a time for families to get together for a lamb dinner, organise egg hunts for children, and eat chocolate.

 Easter Monday (Le Lundi de Pâques)
Easter Monday is the day after Easter and is a public holiday.

*See February for **Carnival** and **Mardi Gras** which can fall in February or March.*

APRIL

Avril

April Fool or April Fish?

Watch your Back on the 1st of April

In many countries, the first day of April is a day to play harmless practical jokes on family and friends. This usually consists of telling a far-fetched story in such a way that it sounds as though it could be true. When the other person falls for our joke, we exclaim, "April fool!" and have a laugh. In France, they play the same sort of jokes, but instead of saying, "April fool!" they say, "*Poisson d'avril!*" which translates as "April fish!" One of the favourite April fish jokes among French children is to tape a paper fish to someone's back without them knowing it.

To find out what fish have to do with these jokes, we have to go back to 1564 to the time of Charles IX (or Charlie 9, as we like to call him). Up until this time, the new year in France was celebrated in the spring, but it had no fixed date. It could be celebrated at different times in different parts of the country, but in most places the new year began at the end of March or the first of April.

It was a time when people would bring out their new spring clothes, get all dressed up, and go out into the fields to celebrate the reawakening of nature – the start of a brand new year. It was customary during these festivities to exchange small gifts, usually food and often fish. Why fish? Maybe it was because the fish is the last sign of the zodiac and the sign for this time of year. Or perhaps because it was during the time of Lent when meat was forbidden and people ate seafood instead. Whatever the reason, fish was a popular New Year's gift.

When young Charlie 9 travelled around his kingdom and saw the different dates for these New Year's celebrations, he wanted to pull his country together. He wanted to get everyone singing "Auld Lang Syne" (or the French equivalent) on the same date. But the date he chose was the 1st of January. The new year would no longer be celebrated in the spring, but in the winter.

Some of Charlie's subjects, especially in the rural regions, didn't hear about the date change and others just didn't want to change their traditions, so they kept their spring celebration. Others felt obliged to comply with the King's new rules and moved their merry-making to January. However, even though they changed the date of their festivities, they kept their time-honoured traditions. They donned their new lightweight spring garments and went out into the icy fields to commemorate the new year. Since it was freezing cold, it's no surprise that many of them fell sick and some of them even died.

Those who survived the first January New Year's observance probably felt pretty silly about wearing their spring
frocks out in the winter, and from then on they wore nice
warm coats. Perhaps to make themselves feel a bit less fool-
ish, they decided to play tricks on the people who still
thought the new year started in the spring. Instead of giving a traditional gift of fish, they would attach a small fish
to the back of someone's clothes with a hook. These little
fish were normally not very fresh and, with the clothes of
that time being more ample, the fish could go unnoticed
for a while. When the person smelled something fishy and
finally found the little stinker stuck to his back, someone
would announce, "It's a *poisson d'avril!*" or "It's an April
fish!" – and that is why these jokes are called April fish and
why fish are associated with the 1st of April.

Thankfully, French children today use paper fish and stick them on unsuspecting backs with tape. The French newspapers like to join in the fun too, and print outrageous stories as April Fool's jokes.

> *Pee-yew!* Something smells fishy!
>
> *Ha ha!* April Fish!

A few April fish hoaxes in French newspapers
from recent years

- Because of budget cuts, the mayor of Paris has decided to sell the Eiffel Tower to Qatar.
- An app called i-FastChef can now be downloaded to turn your Ipad into a hot plate.
- Samsung UK unveiled a new program called Fli-Fy in which small routers attached to pigeons in London will permit WiFi access throughout the city.

April Dates and Events

 1st April – April Fool's Day (Le Premier Avril)
The 1st day of April is a day for practical jokes. The favourite among French children is to stick a paper fish on someone's back without them knowing about it. When it's discovered, they shout, "*Poisson d'avril*" or "April fish"!

---

*See March for **Easter** which can sometimes fall in April.

Note:
After Charlie 9 changed the beginning of the calendar year to the 1st of January, Pope Gregory XIII extended it to all of Christianity. So all countries that celebrate New Year's Day on the 1st day of January have Charlie 9 to thank for it.

MAY

Mai

Give a Flower to Someone you Love

May Day

In France at the end of April, you will see lily-of-the-valley flowers begin to appear as decorations in shop windows and in florist shops. Then on the 1st of May, you might see these flowers being sold on the streets. If you have French friends, you might even receive a sprig as a gift. The long-standing association of this flower with the first day of May has quite an interesting history, and it involves Charlie 9 again. After changing the date of the New Year's celebration and freezing off some of his subjects, he's about to kill more of his citizens with his kindness.

The first day of May is a public holiday in France. It's called *la Fête du Travail*, and it's the equivalent of Labour Day in some other countries – but more on this later. It's also another special day, *la Fête du Muguet* (pronounced something like "mew-gay"), the celebration of the flower known in English as lily-of-the-valley. On the 1st of May, the French offer a sprig of these perfumed nodding bells to those they love, their family and friends.

Where did this delightful tradition originate? Well, we can trace it back to the Middle Ages and to a king who was known for one of the bloodiest religious massacres in France's history: Charles IX (or Charlie 9) who ordered the St. Bartholomew's Day Massacre, in which thousands of Protestants were murdered.

Well, that makes him sound like a pretty terrible guy, but surely he must have had a kinder and gentler side. Let's go back to when little Charlie was nine years old and much nicer. It was 1560 and, in the French countryside, it was customary to give a sprig or branch of some kind of flower on the first day of May. It was meant to chase away the curse of winter and to represent a wish for a fortunate and happy new season. That year, young Charlie was on a visit to the Drôme (an area in south-east France) when he was presented with a sprig of lily-of-the-valley. He was delighted by the gesture and the charming, fragrant flowers.

The next year on the first day of May, when Charlie was ten years old and about to be crowned as Charles IX, king of France, he decided to give a sprig of the same flower to all the ladies of the court. And so the lovely practice of handing out lily-of-the-valley flowers on the first day of May took root.

On the first day of May,
I offer this bouquet -
May it bring you
happiness and
good fortune.

From your king,
Charlie 9

May 1, 1561

Charlie had inherited a kingdom that was devastated by the Wars of Religion, which continued throughout his reign. Toward the end of his time on the throne (and his short life – he died at twenty-three), he was moved by compassion to do something to help his people who were suffering and hungry. He thought about it for a few days and then came up with a great idea: just what the people needed to lift their spirits. On the first day of May, he ordered his soldiers to hand out sprigs of lily-of-the-valley on the streets of Paris as a symbol of good luck and happiness to the people from their king.

Charlie was sure this gesture of goodwill would cheer up his subjects. But the people were hungry and they decided to add the flowers to their soup. Unfortunately, lily-of-the-valley is toxic if eaten, and many of Charlie's subjects died from eating his gift.

Even though the flower wasn't so lucky for Charlie's subjects, the plant somehow managed to maintain its reputation as a bearer of good fortune. However, the tradition of giving it to friends on the first day of May was not widespread until the turn of the twentieth century, when the Parisian fashion designers revived the practice by presenting all their female clients and employees with the symbolic flowers on the 1st of May 1900. Since then, it has become customary throughout France to give a sprig of lily-of-the-valley on the 1st of May to those you hold near and dear.

So, if you're in France on the 1st of May and someone offers you a sprig of lily-of-the-valley – DON'T EAT IT! Just enjoy its beauty and fragrance and bask in the assurance that you are loved... unless, of course, they tell you it would make a nice addition to your soup!

Note:
The first day of May is a day for giving out lily-of-the-valley flowers, as we saw in the previous story, but it's also a day when anyone is allowed to sell these flowers on the street. For this day only, no licence is required and the earnings from selling these flowers are tax free. You just have to be a reasonable distance from the nearest florist, and the flowers must have been picked in the wild or from a garden (preferably from your own).

There is, however, another reason why the first day of May is important. In France, it's called la Fête du Travail *and here, as in many countries, it's the International Day of Workers, or Labour Day. This observance started in 1886 in Chicago, USA with workers lobbying for a five-day/forty-hour working week – instead of the six-day/sixty-hour one that existed at the time. The US has since changed its Labor Day to September, but in much of Europe it's still celebrated on the original date of the 1st of May.*

In France, it's a day for unions to march in the streets. People carry signs proclaiming their grievances or simply march to show their solidarity with one another. It's a public holiday and most people have the day off work.

How many Children does it Take?

Mother's Day

In France, *la Fête des Mères* (or Mother's Day) didn't start out as a day to honour all mothers for their selfless devotion to their families. No, it actually evolved from a government plan designed to motivate women to have more babies. In the late 1800s, the French government was concerned by the country's low birth rate and was looking for ways to remedy this problem.

In 1906, Artas (a small town in the Rhône-Alpes region) took action and held the first recognised celebration of motherhood in France. While they hadn't yet thought of dedicating a special day to mothers, this community decided to give women an example of what being a good patriotic mother looked like. That first year, they awarded two certificates for *Haut Mérite Maternel*, or High Maternal Merit, to two local women who each had nine children. That's right: to be considered a mother of merit took nine children! Other local governments thought this was a good idea and followed suit, honouring only mothers with many children. They were sure this would result in larger families.

Inspired by these regional awards, a national award was created in 1920. There was still no Mother's Day, but French mothers across the land who had raised, *in a dignified manner*, numerous children were awarded a medal. It was called the *Médaille d'Honneur de la Famille Française*, or the Medal of Honour of the French Family. It had three levels, which were determined by the number of children raised. A bronze medal was awarded for four or five children. A silver one could be earned with six or seven, but to "go for the gold" you had to have at least eight children. What an incentive!

The first official Mother's Day (of sorts) was created in the 1920s and was a day to distribute those bronze, silver and gold medals. But the idea was still to acknowledge only women with more than four children. This observance was called *la Fête des Mères de Familles Nombreuses*, or "Mothers of Large Families Day".

Finally in 1941, the Vichy government, under Marshall Pétain, decided to make the holiday all-inclusive and honour all mothers, regardless of the number of children they had. No longer did mothers of only one, two, or three children have to feel inferior or left out. At this point, the holiday began to be widely celebrated. Children were encouraged to show their love and respect to their mothers. Flyers were printed up with advice from Marshall Pétain advising children what they should do for Mother's Day.

It was also at this time, and at Marshall Pétain's urging, that another great French tradition began: teachers started to help schoolchildren make gifts for their mother in honour of her special day. This is where those lovely and coveted Mother's Day macaroni necklaces come in.

———

Note:
The French government is still interested in large families, and the Medal of Honour of the French Family still exists – although it has changed a bit over the years. It's now called the Médaille de la Famille, *or Family Medal, and there are no longer different levels based on number of children. Only the bronze medal is awarded, and it only takes four children to qualify. This medal,*

as the revised name suggests, is no longer reserved just for women; men can qualify too. At some point the government must have figured out that men are also participants in making those babies.

MOTHER'S DAY
25 May, 1941

Your mum has done everything for you...
THE MARSHALL
Asks you to thank her very nicely.

THINK OF THE NICEST SURPRISE THAT YOU CAN, ONE THAT WILL MAKE HER HAPPY.

GIVE HER SOME FLOWERS that you have picked

OR AN OBJECT that you made just for her

MAKE HER A DRAWING as beautiful as you can

WORK HARD IN SCHOOL to take home good grades

DON'T FIGHT with your brothers and sisters

DO YOUR CHORES without having to be asked

HELP WITH THE HOUSEWORK wearing a smile

MEMORISE A LOVELY POEM

WORK = FAMILY = COUNTRY

May Dates and Events

May is a month filled with holidays, and a month when not much business is carried out. It has two fixed holidays and there are two movable ones that often fall in May. This means that it's possible to have four holidays in May – one for each week.

 1st May – May Day or Labour Day
(*Le Premier Mai ou La Fête du Travail*)
The 1st of May is a public holiday and most businesses are closed.

 8th May – Victory Day (*La Fête de la Victoire*)
La Fête de la Victoire is a public holiday which celebrates the victory and the end of the Second World War in Europe in 1945.

May (last Sunday) – Mother's Day
(*La Fête des Mères*)
Mother's Day is an observance normally held on the last Sunday in May. If, however, it happens to fall on the same day as Pentecost, it moves to the first Sunday in June.

The following holidays depend upon the date of Easter but they often fall in May:

Ascension (*L'Ascension*)
Ascension is a religious and public holiday that changes date from year to year. It's celebrated the Thursday forty days after Easter. It's usually in May but can occur from the 30th April to the 3rd June. Since it's a public holiday which falls on a Thursday, the French like to *faire le pont* or "make the bridge" and take Friday off as well, for a nice long four-day weekend.

Pentecost and the day after –
(*Pentecôte et le Lundi de Pentecôte*)
Pentecost falls on the seventh Sunday after Easter and is a religious holiday. But le *Lundi de Pentecôte*, the Monday after Pentecost, is a public holiday.

JUNE

Juin

Fathers Light Up

Father's Day

As we saw in the month of May, the first effort in France to celebrate motherhood was in 1906 (even if it was only for mothers who had *eight* children). But what about fathers? It takes two to make those babies, you know.

In the United States, the first Father's Day celebration was in 1910, but it really took off in the 1930s when it started to be celebrated on the third Sunday of June.

One clever French businessman came up with an idea to give French fathers the recognition they rightfully deserved – and increase his business profits at the same time. His name was Marcel Quercia and his family owned a business called Flaminaire which produced cigarette lighters. In 1949, when his company started to manufacture the first gas lighters, he aimed all his advertising funds at Father's Day.

Even though Father's Day didn't exist in France at the time, he made little rhyming slogans that basically said, "What does your dad want for Father's Day? One of our lighters, of course." Then he gave the date when everyone should honour their father with a new lighter. He went with the American date, the third Sunday of June. And he didn't mess about with honouring only fathers with lots of children – no, every father deserved to have one of his lighters.

His advertising campaign was effective, and children all over France bought his lighters so their fathers could light up those cigarettes (that they didn't know were so bad for them).

Nowadays, young French children make Father's Day gifts at school just like they do for their mums on Mother's Day. They wouldn't want Dad to be jealous of Mum's macaroni necklace, so they make him an accessory as well – a paper tie. Now when they get dressed up to go out for dinner, Mum and Dad will both have something nice to wear.

French Jazz
Fans Outsmart
Hitler

Traditional French Music?

France has a special place in its heart for jazz, and in the summer, you'll find jazz festivals all over the country. In fact, the world's first international jazz festival was held in Nice, France in 1948. But France's relationship with this music started some thirty years earlier during the First World War.

African-American soldiers introduced France to jazz during World War I. After the war, this lively new sound was the perfect accompaniment to *les années folles*, or "the crazy years" of the 1920s, when all art forms were changing and tastes turned to the unconventional and exotic. This new music made people feel alive again: just what was needed after the horrors of the First World War.

Jazz was especially appreciated by the young, and in the early 1930s, a group of Parisian students formed a jazz club. At first they just met to listen to the music, but later they became ambassadors of this new sound. The *Hot Club de France* quickly grew into an important organisation working to promote jazz in France. Hugues Panassié was president and Charles Delaunay secretary, but in 1936 Louis Armstrong was elected honorary president of the club and held that title until his death in 1971.

With the help of the Hot Club, jazz took root in France. Although they appreciated the American jazz groups, the Hot Club was on the lookout for French talent. They "discovered" guitarist Django Reinhardt and violinist Stéphane Grappelli who, along with others, became known as the *Hot Club Quintet*, the first "all-French" jazz band (even though Django was Belgian).

When the Second World War was declared, most of the African American jazz musicians left France – and the French bands were worried. To put it mildly, *Hitler wasn't a jazz fan*. He considered it a tool of the Jews and detrimental to society.

But Hitler wasn't as iron-fisted in France as he was in other countries. He wanted to remain on good terms with the French and use their resources for his war effort. He also planned to make Paris a recreation centre for his troops, so he encouraged the entertainment industry there. Foreign tunes were absolutely forbidden, but he allowed traditional music, thinking his propaganda would be better accepted if it was broadcast along with popular songs.

The Hot Club took advantage of this loophole and set about creating a "French history" for jazz, proclaiming it a traditional French form of music. They held conferences explaining how jazz had been directly inspired by Debussy, an influential French composer of the late 19th and early 20th centuries, and circulated flyers detailing this invented pedigree.

They wrote books to convince Hitler and the Vichy regime of the merits of French jazz. One music critic published a book explaining how jazz was intrinsically French and how it could become the new European music under the Nazi regime. Hugues Panassié, president of the Hot Club, published a book addressing the Vichy regime's argument that jazz couldn't carry a patriotic message. In his book he claimed that

Louis Armstrong disguised as a French man

(beret)

jazz had simply been misunderstood, and he scattered Biblical passages and political quotes throughout the pages to make it sound convincing.

Music experts pointed out that the jazz musicians of the time were all French (because the American musicians had left at the start of the war), and they made "adjustments" to make jazz seem more French. The titles of songs were changed to French: "St Louis Blues" became "Tristesse de St Louis" and "I Got Rhythm" became "Agate Rhythm". The names of composers were either left out or changed. Louis Armstrong's songs were credited to Jean Sablon (a French songwriter) during that time. When they had finished with it, jazz looked as French as baguettes and brie. Their efforts paid off when the Nazis banned subversive "American swing" but permitted traditional "French jazz". Of course, it was the same music, just cleverly repackaged.

Hot Club members weren't just defying the Nazis with music; many of them were active members of the Resistance. They used jazz concerts and conferences as cover to pass information to England. In 1943 the Hot Club headquarters in Paris were raided and some of its officials were arrested. Delaunay, Hot Club secretary, was released after a month, but several of the others perished in concentration camps.

Jazz, however, survived the war and kept the French company during the Nazi Occupation. And when the war was over, France remained faithful to the music – which, by that time, really had become woven into French culture.

Hitler says **NO** to American swing but **YES** to French jazz!

(Don't tell him, but they are the same thing!)

June Dates and Events

 June (3rd Sunday) – Father's Day (*La Fête des Pères*)
A day to honour fatherhood.

 21st June – World Music Day (*La Fête de la Musique*)
This is an all-night music festival on the shortest night of the year. Celebrations are held in many French cities.

JULY

Juillet

Pierre the Patriot Takes Down the Bastille

14th July - La Fête Nationale

The national holiday in France is officially known as *La Fête Nationale*, but is simply called *le quatorze juillet* (the 14th July) most of the time. In English it's referred to as Bastille Day because it was on this date in 1789 that the Parisians stormed the Bastille, a prison that had become a symbol of tyranny and oppression. It also contained the gunpowder they needed to start their revolution – so they stormed it.

Among those doing the storming that day was 34-year-old Pierre-François Palloy (pronounced a bit like pal-wah) who ran a successful Parisian building construction business. After the Bastille was taken, many men climbed onto the towers in a sort of eighteenth-century victory dance, and Pierre was among them. As he stood at the top of that prison and looked down at the angry crowd, he sensed that this was a historic moment and he wanted to be part of it. More accurately, he wanted to be in charge of it.

Pierre started to tear off some of the top stones, and others followed suit. Well, that's his version anyway. Others also claim to have taken down the first stone. But, regardless of who was first, Pierre was a man of action. The next day, he pulled his crew of workmen off all other projects and started the demolition of the Bastille. Many other Parisians were also there to do as much damage as they could to that hated symbol.

Then it occurred to Pierre that he might want to get some kind of authorisation to tear down this monumental building. The following morning, while his crew was chipping away, he presented himself at City Hall, not only to ask permission to tear down the Bastille, but also to be in charge of the entire project.

The newly formed Assembly was debating whether the Bastille should be reused or demolished. Pierre presented his case for its demolition and for his appointment as supervisor. He promised his attention to detail, his determination, his dedication, and his loyalty. He reminded them of his construction company, and he promised to hire only good and patriotic workers. Pierre hung around all day reminding them why he was the best man for the job.

The committee considered the facts: the Bastille was already being torn down, and they had a contractor in front of them who wanted to supervise it. They decided the demolition of the Bastille should continue, under the direction of Pierre Palloy.

Pierre was thrilled. He considered himself the director of the greatest patriotic project that existed. He had an emblem painted on his carriage depicting the storming of the Bastille, and he decorated everything, from his business cards to his account books, with symbols of patriotism. From then on, he signed his name as "Palloy, Patriote", taking "Patriot" as his title.

Pierre the Patriot got what he had wanted and that turned out to be a huge pile of rocks. The Bastille was a big building that turned into an impressive pile of rubble. And, as is often the case, the contractor was in charge of debris disposal.

Some of the larger stones were used in the construction of the Concorde Bridge and other building projects around the city. Many Parisians took stones to make repairs to their homes or just as good-luck pieces. But all this didn't even make a dent in the gigantic pile of rubble that the prison produced. It would take some imagination to dispose of it all and, luckily, Pierre the Patriot had bucketloads of that.

Where most saw rubble, Pierre saw … patriotic souvenirs. He would make, sell and give away souvenirs. They would all bear his name, of course, and tell the story of his patriotic endeavour.

He set up a factory on another site he owned in Paris where carving and engraving would be done. His first project was to make eighty-three models of the Bastille, carved from the prison's stones. They were given to each of the eighty-three newly formed districts. These were not little trinkets to put on the mantelpiece; they were grand representations of a grand project. The models were 1.37 metres long by 1.2 metres tall (4.5 feet long by 4 feet tall) and were delivered by a group of specially chosen, young, good-looking, patriotic men called "Apostles of Liberty". Pierre wrote a speech which they had to memorise and then recite at the presentation of the gifts.

Along with the model of the Bastille, the Apostles of Liberty bore other gifts: a paving stone from the dungeon, a plan and description of the building, a ball and chain, a piece of armour found in the prison, and a painting. Each department received three crates of Bastille debris (I mean ...souvenirs).

Pierre still had a lot of rock as well as iron, wood, marble, etc. He transformed these materials into all sorts of items, including medallions, statues, snuff-boxes, paperweights, candy dishes, inkwells and jewellery. These souvenirs were sent all over France, Europe – even to the Americas. Almost every organisation, administration, society and public figure received their piece of the Bastille. He made medals for his workers to wear, and he even made boundary stones to mark the borders of the "Land of Liberty".

About two and a half years later, when the demolition of the Bastille was finished and most of the debris had been repurposed as souvenirs and scattered around the world, Pierre held a ceremony with lots of pomp where he delivered his meticulously kept accounts to the committee. They checked and approved them and everyone went on their merry way.

However, a few years later, under a new government, Pierre the Patriot was arrested and charged with embezzlement. He was only held for two months, but while in prison he asked his wife to arrange to have one of the stones from the Bastille brought into his cell. He even continued to fill orders for Bastille souvenirs that came in during his short incarceration.

In the end, Pierre's patriotism was acknowledged. He was exonerated and in 1814 he received the *Décoration du Lys* award for his patriotic service. It seems only fitting that Pierre, whose name means stone, is remembered for his imaginative methods of scattering stones from the Bastille to every corner of France and beyond.

Some interesting Bastille facts

- The largest key to the Bastille was sent to George Washington, the first president of the United States, and delivered by General La Fayette.
- The story of *The Man in the Iron Mask* is set in the Bastille and based on a real mystery prisoner who wore a black velvet mask.
- When the revolutionaries took the Bastille, there were only seven prisoners inside: four forgers, two insane, and one nobleman imprisoned at the request of his family. The others had been transferred or released shortly before. The revolutionaries were so disappointed that they invented a prisoner – an old man in chains confined to a dark pit for years. He was to represent all those who had been wrongfully imprisoned there

July Dates and Events

14th July – National Holiday
(*La Fête Nationale ou Le Quatorze Juillet*)
The national holiday in France is known simply as
le quatorze juillet (the 14th July). It's *not* called
Bastille Day in France. It's celebrated all over the country
with fireworks.

Summer Sales (*Les Soldes*)
The second round of sales normally starts at the
end of June and lasts most of July. They run for five
weeks. Just like the winter ones, these sale dates are
regulated by the government. These two sales events
(summer and winter) are the main sales of the year.

AUGUST

Août

The Long Vacations

July and August Holidays

The French love their holidays, and they know how to make the most of them, as I mentioned earlier. But July and August are special, they are the months of *les grandes vacances*, or the "long vacations". Most people take a two or three-week holiday in either July or August. Those who vacation in July are called *juillettists* (pronounced jwee-yeah-teest) and those who take August holidays are called *aoûtiens* (pronounced ah-oo-sian). For the sake of simplicity, we'll call them Julyists and Augustians.

With everyone on holiday, business really slows down in July and is almost non-existent in August (except for tourism, of course). So if you are in France and need to get some kind of administrative paperwork done during these months, don't frustrate yourself – just relax and go to the beach with everyone else, because nothing is going to get done until September.

However, business didn't always grind to a halt in July and August. Before 1936 few people, other than government employees, had paid time off. Then in 1936 there were general strikes throughout France and one of the workers' demands was for a paid holiday. The government finally decided that it was healthy for people to have a few weeks off work to relax, and that their work would improve because of it.

On the 20th of June 1936, a law was passed that gave every salaried employee two weeks of paid leave. A few weeks later, on the 1st of August, all salaried employees were on holiday. For many, it was for the first time in their lives.

They went to the countryside and the seaside. Initially, these overworked French people weren't sure what one did on holiday, so they just watched the rich for a while and started to imitate them. They were fast learners and soon they were sitting in the sun drinking cool drinks. They were getting the hang of vacationing and they liked it.

In the 1950s, when a third week of holiday time was added and automobiles were widely owned, the French started packing up their cars and travelling across the country (mostly heading south) for their "long vacations". This was the birth of mass tourism, and inevitably led to the first "long traffic jams".

In the 1960s, a fourth week of vacation time was added, then in the 1980s a fifth. As holidays grew longer, workers were often given a choice of when to take their time off. They divided into two camps: those who took their breaks in July and those who vacationed in August. Today, July and August are still the preferred holiday months for many. Consequently, every year, the weekend with the biggest traffic jams is at the end of July when the Julyists who are returning home cross paths with the Augustians who are leaving to go on holiday. These massive jams are called the *chassé-croisé* (after a dance where partners continually cross in front of each other).

Of course, not everyone participates in this dance because not everyone gets paid time off. It only applies to salaried employees, so those who are self-employed or not in a salaried position don't get paid holidays. Furthermore, not all employees get to choose the date of their holiday. Some businesses (almost 40%) close for the month of August and all their employees have no choice but to be Augustians.

But for those who are salaried and do have a holiday choice, it seems that their choice might say something about their outlook on life and work. In the larger companies, at least, some stereotypes have developed over the years for these two groups, with Augustians being seen as putting work before pleasure and the Julyists as just wanting to have fun.

But times are changing and the old stereotypes aren't as valid as they once might have been. Fewer people are taking long holidays and many factors enter into their choice of dates. Nonetheless, July and August remain the favourite months for the "long vacations" and there are still those who are very attached to their preferred month.

The Julyists and the Augustians may disagree on the best month to take a holiday, but they do agree on the best location. The largest percentage of both groups prefer to holiday at the seaside.

And there is one other point on which they can agree: people who take their holidays in September are really odd!

Augustian vs Julyist

I'm dedicated to my job. I take my holiday when business is slowest and at the same time as my boss.

He's a *lèche-botte*, a "boot-licker", trying to score points with the boss.

He doesn't take work seriously. He's the first to leave and when he comes back in August, there's nothing to do.

There's more to life than work, it's meant to be enjoyed. I'll be back in August when everyone else is on holiday (and there's not much to do).

August Dates
and Events

Besides being a month of long vacations, August has one public holiday.

15th August – The Assumption
(L'Assomption ou Le Quinze Août)
This public holiday is usually known as le *quinze août* (the 15th August). It's one of the Catholic holidays that has gained public holiday status. Those who don't take their vacation days in August always hope this holiday will fall on a Tuesday or Thursday so they can *faire le pont* (make the bridge) and take a long, four-day weekend.

SEPTEMBER

Septembre

Tooth Fairy
versus
Tooth Mouse

Traditional Tooth Collectors

When children start to lose their baby (milk) teeth, it's an important milestone in their lives, so it's not surprising that traditions have sprung up around this event. In many countries there is a folkloric character who comes in the night and takes away the tooth. Let's compare the one who presides over baby teeth in many Anglophone countries with the one who is responsible for France.

First, we'll discuss the Tooth Fairy. In some parts of the world, it's a fairy who's in charge of collecting fallen baby teeth. When a child loses a tooth, he tucks it under his pillow when he goes to bed at night. While he's sleeping, a cute little fairy (normally wearing a pink tutu and carrying a twinkling magic wand) flies into the room. She flits onto the bed, gently lifts the pillow under the sleeping child's head, and ever so delicately takes the tooth. She doesn't steal it though. No, she leaves a nice shiny coin in its place. Most children consider this a pretty good exchange.

France, however, doesn't seem to be in the Tooth Fairy's territory. Or maybe it's just too far for her little wings to carry her but, for whatever reason, she doesn't visit this part of the world. What happens, then, when French children lose their teeth? Do they still get compensated?

Yes, indeed they do. When they lose a tooth, the process starts in pretty much the same way. They put the fallen tooth under their pillow at night, just like the other children do. But who sneaks into their room at night to take the tooth and leave a coin? That would be *La Petite Souris*, or "the Little Mouse". That's right, a MOUSE! French parents allow a mouse to crawl into their child's bed, wiggle its way under the pillow, and take the tooth! Of course, the Little Mouse, like the Tooth Fairy, leaves a coin in place of the tooth.

Where does this rodent tradition come from? It seems that it can be traced back to a seventeenth century French fairytale by Madame d'Aulnoy, called *La Bonne Petite Souris* or "The Good Little Mouse". However, the French parents who tell their children about the nice little mouse that will crawl into their bed at night and take their tooth have surely never read this story – because this little mouse really wasn't so good. Well, I suppose in one sense you could say she was good, because she did help the people get rid of a very evil king. But the way she went about it was anything but nice.

As it turns out, the "good little mouse" in the book is actually a fairy. (Maybe she's related to the Tooth Fairy – the one in the pink tutu.) But this little pixie turns into a mouse at night and creeps up into the evil king's bed. While he sleeps, she bites one ear. He turns over and she bites the other. He screams in pain and calls everyone in the castle to search for the mouse. In the meantime the "good little mouse" scurries into the room of the equally evil prince and does the same thing to him. Then back to the once-again-sleeping king to bite his nose. There is more screaming and mouse-searching while the "good little mouse" is nibbling on the princely nose. When everyone is called to the prince's chamber to search for her, she goes back to the king and into his mouth, where she chews on his tongue, cheeks and lips. Then of course, she does the same to the prince.

The "good little mouse" in this story causes a lot of havoc in the royal beds, but she doesn't take any teeth and she doesn't leave any money. Well, once she did actually cause the king to lose four teeth when she pushed him out of a tree. But she wasn't in mouse form – she was invisible at the time.

In any case, *la Petite Souris* is apparently in much better humour these days and, of course, since French children are all good and well-behaved, she wouldn't dare do any of these awful things to them. But still, no matter how nice they say she is, she's still a MOUSE!

September Dates and Events

 September (3rd weekend) – Heritage Days
(*Les Journées du Patrimoine*)
During this weekend, the public is invited to visit many cultural sites that aren't normally open to the public. Museums, historic buildings, etc. might be open at a reduced fee or perhaps even free of charge.

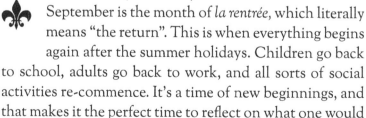

The Return (*La Rentrée*)
September is the month of *la rentrée*, which literally means "the return". This is when everything begins again after the summer holidays. Children go back to school, adults go back to work, and all sorts of social activities re-commence. It's a time of new beginnings, and that makes it the perfect time to reflect on what one would

like to accomplish or improve in the "new year". Many French people make a list of resolutions at this time, just as they do in January.

OCTOBER

Octobre

A Girl Called Fanny that No One Wants to Kiss

Pétanque - A Traditional Sport

Pétanque is a form of boules that is played all over France, but is especially popular in the south. There's a famous scene in one of Marcel Pagnol's films, that shows a tram being stopped because a game of pétanque has spilled over onto the tracks. The game is so important that the passengers simply have to wait until it has finished before continuing their journey.

In the sport of pétanque, a small ball called the *cochonnet*, or "little pig", is thrown out first. Then the players throw their balls, trying to get them as close as possible to the *cochonnet*. Of course, the rules are more complicated than that but, basically, points are allocated based on the close-ness of each player's ball to the *cochonnet*, and the first team to reach thirteen points wins. And this is where the girl called Fanny comes in.

The original Fanny was a kind-hearted young lady who worked in a café near a pétanque court in the mid-1800s. Whenever a team suffered the humiliation of losing a game 13-0 (meaning that they had scored no points during the entire game), her heart would go out to them and, to ease their pain, she would allow each of them to kiss her on the cheek.

One day, the mayor of the village was playing pétanque outside the café and he was having a really bad day. His team lost the game 13-0 and he went to Fanny to be con-soled. But for some reason, she despised this mayor and, instead of offering him her cheek to kiss, she stepped up onto a chair, bent over and lifted her skirt. Can't you just hear her saying, "You can kiss this!" The mayor was sur-prised, but he was up to the challenge and, to the amuse-ment of everyone, two loud kisses rang out through the café.

The next time a team lost 13-0 and went to see Fanny for consolation, they declined her offer to kiss her lovely face. They wanted to plant a kiss in the same place as the mayor! Good-naturedly, she agreed, and soon that was the pre-ferred kissing location for all defeated teams. This new custom quickly spread throughout the world of pétanque, and women all over France carried on the tradition estab-lished by the first sympathetic young pétanque supporter called Fanny.

But at some point there was a shortage of compassionate female fans willing to continue this practice and the pétanque clubs had to resort to posters or sculptures representing Fanny. In almost every clubhouse you will find an image of a woman's bare bottom, honouring the memory of that heroine of pétanque. She hangs patiently on the wall, waiting to console the heavy-hearted defeated ones. In remembrance of the original pétanque groupie, her name has been given to the act of losing 13-0. Those who find themselves in that sad situation are said to "kiss Fanny" or "to be Fanny".

The ceremony of "kissing Fanny" is still observed today. Sometimes a bell is rung to announce the shameful loss and to call others to come and watch the proceedings. The losers, often on their knees, have to kiss Fanny (or her representation) and then they normally have to buy drinks for everyone – because "Fanny pays!"

And this is how a very traditional French sport pays homage to one young lady and her unusual contribution to the game.

October Dates
and Events

31st October – Halloween

Halloween is relatively new to France, first appearing in the 1990s. It's sometimes acknowledged in shop window decorations, and sometimes there are fancy-dress (costume) parties for children, but it's not widely celebrated.

NOVEMBER

Novembre

Truffle Hunting in Provence

Finding the Finicky Fungus

Truffle season in Provence starts in mid-November and runs through mid-March. But what exactly are truffles and how does one go about finding them?

A truffle, according to the Oxford Dictionary, is "a strong-smelling underground fungus that resembles an irregular, rough-skinned potato, growing chiefly in broadleaved woodland on calcareous soils." Now doesn't that just sound delicious?

It makes you want to run right out into a "broadleaved woodland on calcareous soil" to find one, doesn't it? Ah, but that's the problem. Finding truffles can be tricky business. They grow underground on the roots of other plants, mostly oak trees (in a broadleaved woodland) but basically, truffles grow where they want and only when the conditions suit them (in calcareous, or chalky soil). Fortunately, they usually find Provence to be a suitable area. But since they are underground and can't be seen, it's best to enlist the help of a very sensitive nose to help find them.

The original and best truffle-sniffers were pigs; female pigs to be exact. It seems that the scent of this little fungus resembles male pig hormones, so the females are eager to find it. The problem with truffle-hunting pigs is that they are big, hard to control and they really like the taste of truffles.

Today, dogs are normally used for the truffle hunt. It seems they are easier to train and control than pigs. Even though dogs are not naturally attracted to the smell of truffles, they can be taught to hunt for them. Small dogs are usually the best choice, because they are easier to handle and easier to get the truffle away from than a big dog. These little dogs take their work seriously because every time they find a truffle they get a treat – ideally, one that tastes better than a truffle, so they won't eat the harvest.

Speaking of eating truffles, we have to wonder who first looked at one of these ugly, lumpy things that didn't smell particularly good and decided to take a bite. Well, one legend says that a farmer saw his sow dig up and eat a truffle. He watched her for a few days and, since she didn't die, he decided to try one too. He discovered that this lumpy ball of fungus tasted delicious and added flavour to all his farmhouse recipes. The truffle-eating farmer and his wife, who up until this point had been unable to conceive, went on to have thirteen children. This seems to support the truffle's reputation as an aphrodisiac for people as well as for pigs.

Like the above-mentioned farmer, the ancient Greeks and Romans dined on truffles. But the tasty fungus fell out of favour during the superstitious Middle Ages, when it was associated with witchcraft and devils. These ideas might have come from the truffle's dark, lumpy appearance and the fact that it grows underground. Also, there is often a place on the ground above the truffles where no grass will grow – very spooky! The fact that they were considered aphrodisiacs also made them taboo. Interestingly, however, after the Pope moved to Avignon, right in the heart of truffle territory, truffles became acceptable once again.

During the Renaissance, the truffle's tarnished reputation was fully restored, and by the sixteenth century this delicacy was on the tables of all the nobles in Europe. In the royal court of Turin, Italy, in the 1700s, truffle hunting became a form of entertainment. Aristocratic foreign guests were invited to accompany and observe the royal dogs hunting for truffles. The guests must have worked up an appetite watching those little dogs work, so afterwards they were invited to a royal truffle-tasting consisting of various truffle treats.

Throughout history, truffles have been adored for their taste, coveted for their supposed favourable properties, or banned for their alleged sinister character. They have been eaten and loved by pig-farmers (and their pigs) as well as by popes and kings.

Here are a few of the notable people who had a fondness for this little fungus:

- British poet Lord Byron kept a truffle on his desk

when writing. He thought the scent stimulated his creativity.

- Catherine de Medici, Queen of France in the sixteenth century, who brought refinement to the French table (as well as the fork), is said to have been addicted to them.
- Napoleon Bonaparte ate truffles to give him strength in battle (and in bed). When Napoleon was in need of a successor, one of his officers confided that his own large family was the result of eating truffles, which were plentiful in his region of France. When the officer went home on leave, he came back with a bag full of truffles for the Emperor – and nine months later little Napoleon II came into the world.
- Rasputin prescribed truffles to be eaten by the Russian tsar, Nicholas II, to strengthen his blood and bloodline.
- Alexandre Dumas, author of *The Three Musketeers*, among other works, said of the truffle, "Food lovers in every century have never been able to say the name of the truffle without tipping their hat."

I love truffles more than mud - and I REALLY love mud!

Little Saints of Provence

Extreme Nativity Scenes

In many parts of the world, Nativity scenes are used as Christmas decorations, but in Provence, they are taken to the extreme. The traditional Biblical figures make up only a tiny part of these sprawling displays. In Provence, the whole village is represented in the nativity. You will see the butcher, the baker, the candlestick maker and every other profession that is practised in a French Provençal village. These figurines are called *santons or* "little saints".

The history of the Nativity scene and these "little saints" can be traced back to St Francis of Assisi, who wasn't French but did have a French connection – his mother was from Provence. He was born in Assisi, Italy, while his father was away on business in France. His mother named him Giovanni, but when his father returned, he started calling him Francesco (meaning Frenchman), which is Francis in English.

It seems that St Francis was the first to make a representation of the Nativity. In 1223, he used a little manger (feeding trough) filled with straw and a live donkey and ox as props for his Christmas sermon. Inspired by this, other churches started to display these *crèche* scenes and the custom spread throughout Christendom. The live animals were eventually replaced by figurines of the people and animals mentioned in the Bible. Then, during the French Revolution, which separated the State from the Catholic Church, masses and *crèches* in churches were outlawed. So those who wanted to have a *crèche* started to make their own homemade versions.

Later, little painted figures made of clay (*santons*) began to be produced, making it possible for each household to have its very own Nativity scene. At first, like the ones that had been displayed in the churches, they contained only the traditional Biblical cast of characters. But in Provence, they quickly evolved as more and more craftspeople and tradesmen *santons* were added. Each *santon* is shown with something that identifies his or her trade, and sometimes even with all the paraphernalia needed to carry out their vocations. These figures are passed down from generation to generation and new ones are added each year.

For those looking to enlarge their *crèche*, a *foire aux santons* or "*santon* fair" is the place to go. The first *santon* fair was held in 1803 in Marseilles. Now, you'll see them all over the south of France. At these fairs you can find *santons* of all sizes and shapes. The smallest clay figures start at about 2 centimetres (less than one inch) tall, and the larger, clothed ones are about 30 centimetres (12 inches) tall. Normally *santons* are dressed in eighteenth-century fashion, and while these traditional styles are by far the most popular, there are modern versions as well. Each *santonnier* (*santon* maker) has his or her own style and speciality.

Of course, all those little saints need to be placed in the proper setting. At the *santon* fairs you'll also find buildings, olive trees, animals, streams, bridges, lavender fields – everything that you need to build your town.

The history of the Nativity scene started with St Francis, who was of Provençal heritage, and his simple Christmas display containing an ox, a donkey, and a manger. Today in Provence, his mother's native land, the Christmas *crèche* has been taken to the extreme and now includes every imaginable person, animal, plant and building to be found in a Provençal village. I can't help but think that St Francis's mother would be proud.

Mary, you stay inside with the baby. I'll go out and see what's going on - it looks like an entire French village has turned up!

Of course, Provençal Nativity scenes have the normal Biblical characters, but there are also many who are not mentioned in the Bible. Here is a small sampling of some Provençal characters who attend the Nativity:

- The blind man and his son. The man's oldest son went missing and because of his sadness, he cried so much that he went blind. His youngest son leads him to the crèche.
- The gypsies, who had kidnapped the blind man's son, show up and are moved to return him to his father.
- The "pistachioed" is a farm-hand who is always depicted as a skirt-chaser. Pistachios grow in Provence and are considered an aphrodisiac, thus this man's nickname.
- *Le ravi* or "the delighted one" is a bit like the village idiot and very happy and excited about the

Nativity. He's always shown with his hands in the air and is often accompanied by a female version called *la ravie*.

- The mayor comes to the *crèche*, of course, to record the birth.
- A preacher shows up who seems upset by the whole affair.
- A monk who represents St Francis of Assisi is there. St Francis is the patron saint of the *santonniers*, or *santon* makers.
- A little drummer boy leads a line of dancers in a traditional local dance called the *farandole*.
- An elderly couple always observes the scene while sitting on a bench arm in arm.
- A fisherman arrives with his nets and his wife, the fishmonger.
- A woman brings a pot of snails (escargot).
- A farmwoman is fattening a goose for *foie gras*.
- A farmer makes an appearance and brings along his truffle pig.

And there are many more ...

November Dates and Events

 1st November – All Saints' Day (*La Toussaint*)
This is the day the French take flowers to the graves
of their loved ones. The flowers of choice are
chrysanthemums, which are in bloom at this time
of year. From this custom, the chrysanthemum has gained
the reputation as being the flower for the dead. (According
to tradition, you should not offer chrysanthemums as a
gift to someone who is still alive.)

 11th November – Armistice Day (*Jour d'Armistice*)
Armistice Day is a public holiday that commemo-
rates the Armistice of 1918 and the end of World
War I. It's also a time to remember those who died
in both world wars. There are usually ceremonies
throughout France where wreaths are laid on war memori-
als.

November (3rd Thursday) – Release of *Beaujolais Nouveau*

At one-minute after midnight on the third Thursday of November, the new Beaujolais wine, or *Beaujolais Nouveau*, goes on sale. It's a red wine from the Beaujolais region that is fermented for just a few weeks. Even though the wine may not be sophisticated or great-tasting, it signals the end of the grape harvest and offers yet another reason to celebrate.

DECEMBER

Décembre

Thirteen Desserts and a Log

A Provençal Christmas Eve Tradition

The Christmas season in France is full of traditions and, as with most good traditions, food is usually involved.

In Provence, preparations for the Christmas holiday meals begin on the 4th of December, St Barbara's day, with the planting of wheat (in the kitchen, that is). Wheatgerm is placed in small bowls lined with damp cotton. These dishes will later be placed on the Christmas Eve dinner table or in the nativity *crèche*. If the little green shoots grow tall and strong, the inhabitants can expect a good and prosperous year. If not... well, let's just say, you'd better make sure that you water your wheat sprouts!

The *gros souper* or "big dinner" eaten on Christmas Eve is rich in religious symbolism, and the numbers of everything is very important. Even if some of the religious aspects have been forgotten, the numerical traditions remain.

3

The holiday table is covered by three white tablecloths and holds three candelabras and three dishes of wheat sprouts. After dinner, the desserts stay on the table for three days. The number three represents the Holy Trinity.

7

The meal is made up of seven meatless dishes. Normally a fish plate is served along with six vegetable platters. The number seven represents the seven wounds of Jesus.

13

The dinner is accompanied by thirteen bread rolls and then followed by thirteen desserts. The number thirteen represents Jesus and his twelve disciples.

Thirteen desserts? Yes, you read that correctly, there are *thirteen* desserts and everyone is required to taste each one of them! It comes as no surprise that the different types of dessert are also symbolic.

The Thirteen Christmas Desserts

Desserts 1-4: Four types of dried fruit and nuts, which represent four religious orders (dried figs = Franciscans; almonds = Carmelites; raisins = Dominicans; walnuts (or hazelnuts) = Augustinians).

Desserts 5-6: Two types of nougat: white and black (to represent good and evil).

Dessert 7: A loaf of olive oil flatbread called a *pompe à l'huile* that must be torn off, never cut with a knife (you would risk a year of bad luck).

Dessert 8: Dates, to represent the Orient, the birthplace of Jesus.

Pompe à l'huile:
If you cut me,
you'll be sorry!

Desserts 9-13: While the first eight desserts are traditional, you are free to choose the last five. They normally include a selection of fresh and candied fruit.

To help with the task of assembling all these desserts, there are holiday markets specialising in the required ingredients. You can even buy one box containing all thirteen items.

The Christmas Log

On Christmas Day, there is normally another large meal, often featuring turkey. After that the traditional *bûche de Noël* (Yule log cake) is added to the other thirteen desserts. Yes, another dessert!

Originally, the *bûche de Noël* was a real log. The burning of the Christmas log is an ancient custom which is now practised only by those in possession of a large fireplace. In the olden days, people would search for the biggest log they could find. Ideally, it would come from the trunk of a fruit or olive tree, and was meant to burn for a long time – at least three days or even for a week, until the first of January. Wine or olive oil would be poured over it before it was lit by the oldest member of the family amid wishes for a year of prosperity and happiness.

Yule Log: It looks like a tree trunk...
but tastes so much better!

Since many modern homes and apartments are not equipped for burning tree trunks, what can be done? Well, the obvious solution is to make a cake that looks like a log. Its icing is wavy, to resemble tree bark, and often little almond paste mushrooms and other decorations are added to it. This yummy log cake can count as one of the thirteen Christmas Eve desserts, or it can be introduced after Christmas lunch as dessert number fourteen.

No one knows exactly when eating cake took the place of burning a tree trunk, but what a great idea!

December Dates
and Events

Christmas Markets (*Les Marchés de Noël*)

From the end of November through the first part of January, Christmas markets can be found in many French cities. They are usually made up of little huts housing artisans selling their wares. Many cities also install temporary ice-skating rinks and sometimes carnival-type rides, such as carousels, for children.

25th December – Christmas (*Noël*)

Christmas Day is a public holiday. Families usually celebrate on Christmas Eve with a large family meal called *le réveillon* (or *le gros souper* in Provence) and then they celebrate some more on Christmas Day with lots more food.

31st December – New Year's Eve (*La Saint-Sylvestre*)

Almost every day on the French calendar bears a saint's name, and the 31st of December just happens to be St Sylvestre's day – so New Year's Eve is called *la Saint-Sylvestre*. This saint was a pope who died on 31st December 335, and he had nothing to do with singing "Auld Lang Syne" or kissing at midnight ... as far as we know.

In France, the mistletoe, or *le gui*, is associated with New Year's Eve, and lovers exchange kisses under it at midnight. But no one is opposed to kissing under it the entire holiday season. Mistletoe is linked to good luck and prosperity.

New Year's Eve is often celebrated with a large family dinner, and just like Christmas Eve dinner, it is known as *le réveillon*.

About the Author

Margo Lestz is American by birth but now divides her time between London, England and Nice, France (with a little bit of Florence, Italy thrown in for good measure). Life in a foreign country is never dull and every day is a new learning experience.

She describes herself as a perpetual student and is always taking some kind of course or researching a moment in history that has caught her fancy. She's curious by nature and is always wondering who, what, why, when, where, and how.

Margo shares her adventures (and her questions) with Jeff, her husband of many years.

French Holidays & Traditions is the first in her Curious Histories series. Still to come are histories of Nice, France (her adopted hometown) and women in French history.

Author site: margolestz.com
Blog: curiousrambler.com

Lightning Source UK Ltd.
Milton Keynes UK
UKOW06f2102170615

253687UK00001B/3/P